KT-522-388

CULTURE

in New Zealand

Melanie Guile

Heinemann
LIBRARY

C 04 0042553

www.heinemann.co.uk/library

Visit our website to find out more information about Heinemann Library books.

To order:

☎ Phone 44 (0) 1865 888066

▤ Send a fax to 44 (0) 1865 314091

▭ Visit the Heinemann Bookshop at www.heinemann.co.uk/library to browse our catalogue and order online.

First published 2003 in Australia by Heinemann Library a division of Harcourt Education Australia, 18–22 Salmon Street, Port Melbourne Victoria 3207 Australia (a division of Reed International Books Australia Pty Ltd, ABN 70 001 002 357).

© Reed International Books Australia Pty Ltd 2002
First published in paperback in 2005
The moral right of the publisher has been asserted.

All rights reserved. No part of this publication may be reproduced, stored in a retrieval system or transmitted in any form or by any means electronic, mechanical, photocopying, recording or otherwise without the prior written permission of the publishers or a licence permitting restricted copying in the United Kingdom issued by the Copyright Licensing Agency Ltd, 90 Tottenham Court Road, London W1T 4LP (www.cla.co.uk).

Series cover and text design by Stella Vassiliou
Paged by Stella Vassiliou
Edited by Carmel Heron
Production by Michelle Sweeney

Pre-press by Digital Imaging Group (DIG), Melbourne, Australia
Printed and bound in China by WKT Company Ltd.

ISBN 1 74070 062 7 (hardback)
07 06 05 04 03 02
10 9 8 7 6 5 4 3 2 1

ISBN 0 431 18126 8 (paperback)
09 08 07 06 05
10 9 8 7 6 5 4 3 2 1

British Library Cataloguing in Publication Data
Guile, Melanie.
Culture in New Zealand.
306'.0993
A full catalogue record for this book is available from the British library.

Acknowledgements
Cover photograph of an entrant in the 2000 Wearable Art Awards supplied by Nelson Mail.

Other photographs supplied by: Annelies van der Pol: pp. 6, 11; Australian Picture Library: pp. 7, 9, 16, 19, 21, 24; Bloomfield Furniture: p. 28; Diogenes Designs Ltd.: p. 22; G.R. 'Dick' Roberts Photo Library: p. 14 (both); Michel Tuffery – F.2544/Museum of New Zealand, Te Papa Tongarewa: p. 27; Nelson Mail: p. 17; Peter Robinson – B.036998/Museum of New Zealand, Te Papa Tongarewa: p. 15; Sport. The Library: p. 25; The New Zealand Herald: pp. 23, 29.

Every attempt has been made to trace and acknowledge copyright. Where an attempt has been unsuccessful, the publisher would be pleased to hear from the copyright owner so any omission or error can be rectified in subsequent printings.

Disclaimer
All the Internet addresses (URLs) given in this book were valid at the time of printing. However, due to the dynamic nature of the Internet, some addresses may have changed, or sites may have ceased to exist since publication. While the author and publisher regret any inconvenience this may cause readers, no responsibility for any such changes can be accepted by either the author or the publisher.

WEST DUNBARTONSHIRE LIBRARIES	
C040042553	
CAW	18/02/2005
J306.0993	£6.99
RL	

CONTENTS

Words that appear in bold, **like this**, are explained in the glossary on page 30.

CULTURE IN
New Zealand

❯ Isolated islands

The islands of New Zealand are found in the vast waters of the South Pacific Ocean. They are a long way from the world's main population centres. This **isolation** is central to New Zealand culture. First Maori, then Europeans, found the land and built their communities with little outside help. English settlers took land from the Maori, who fought back to preserve their way of life and to keep their land. Over time, the two cultures established a dynamic partnership that produced the rich and lively mix that New Zealand is today. As in many modern societies, gangs, domestic violence, drug and alcohol problems exist, but with only 3.9 million people, most New Zealanders are proud of their unique and diverse **multicultural** way of life.

❯ What is culture?

Culture is a people's way of living. It is the way people identify themselves as a group, separate and different from any other. Culture includes a group's language, social customs and habits, as well as its traditions of art, craft, dance, music, writing and religion.

New Zealanders see themselves as quite different from other 'western' countries, particularly Australia. They are passionately proud of the rugged beauty of their landscape, their 'clean and green' environment, their open and fair society and the harmony they have achieved among diverse cultural groups. They are renowned for their openness and friendliness, and their ability to make do with what is available, or 'fix it with a length of number 8 wire', as they put it.

Although New Zealand is a small nation, New Zealanders generally view themselves as strong, courageous and independent-minded. This shows in their passion for extreme sports and mountaineering. It is evident in their obsession with the national sport, rugby, a tough game at which they excel. It shows in the way New Zealanders are ready to explore anything new or different in the arts scene, often defying international opinion. And it shows in their stand against the United States of America, refusing American **nuclear-powered** ships entry to its ports. Whether in sport, art or politics, New Zealanders are ready to take on the world – and win.

The flag of New Zealand. The Union Jack in the top left corner shows the country's links with Britain, and the Queen is still the Head of State. However, New Zealand's Prime Minister Helen Clark has said a **republic** is a certainty.

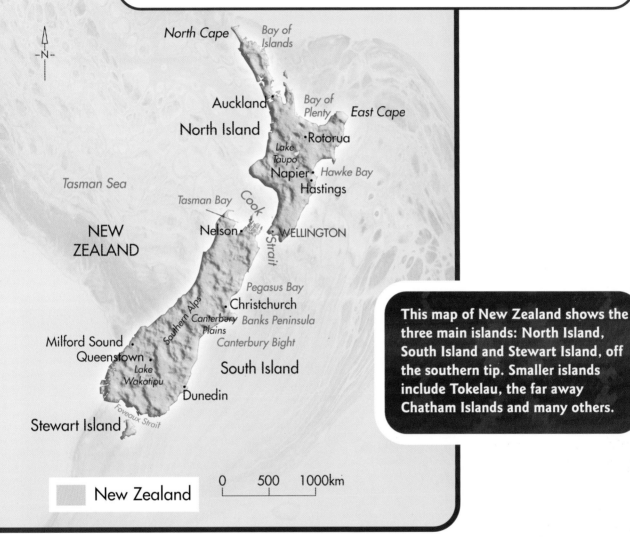

North Cape

Bay of Islands

-N-

Auckland

North Island

Bay of Plenty

East Cape

Rotorua

Lake Taupo

Tasman Sea

Napier

Hawke Bay

Hastings

Tasman Bay

Cook Strait

NEW ZEALAND

Nelson

WELLINGTON

Pegasus Bay

Christchurch

Southern Alps

Canterbury Plains

Banks Peninsula

Canterbury Bight

Milford Sound

Queenstown

Lake Wakatipu

South Island

Dunedin

Foveaux Strait

Stewart Island

New Zealand

0   500   1000km

This map of New Zealand shows the three main islands: North Island, South Island and Stewart Island, off the southern tip. Smaller islands include Tokelau, the far away Chatham Islands and many others.

A wilder side

New Zealand's landscape is beautiful, but it can also be dangerous, with towering mountain wildernesses, active volcanoes, trembling earthquakes and gales that lash the west coast. Isolation also threatens, in a country with only fourteen people per square kilometre. Many New Zealanders meet their country's physical challenges head on with gruelling **endurance races** that pit the individual against the power of the land. The country's artists and writers sometimes capture a brooding mood in their works. Particularly in plays, novels and films, they often present images of loneliness, hardship and isolation.

Race relations

Of New Zealand's total population of nearly four million people, 76 per cent are of European descent, 14 per cent are Maori, five per cent are Pacific Islanders and five per cent are Asian (mainly Indian and Chinese). Unlike other indigenous people around the world, the Maori were recognised as traditional landowners by the British Government. In the famous Treaty of Waitangi, signed by Maori chiefs in 1840, the British promised the Maori people protection from European land-grabbers. But the promises were not kept and, by 1900, much of the best land was taken by whites for farming. Nevertheless, Maori culture proved resilient and customs, arts, crafts and language were preserved. Indeed, in recent decades, there has been a renewed interest in Maori culture in New Zealand.

By the 1970s, many Maori were moving from their traditional lands into the cities, particularly Auckland. At the same time, migrants from the Pacific Islands and Asia added to the racial mix. Auckland now has the largest **Polynesian** population in the world. Most New Zealanders are proud of the efforts they have made to create a vibrant multicultural society.

Traditional Maori culture is incorporated into this performance by the Royal New Zealand Ballet.

True value

A recent survey by economics experts revealed that New Zealanders valued the environment and people's welfare above business success and earning money. Unfazed by the country's poor economic performance, people cited quality of life as much more important.

Maori language, customs, songs and dances are taught in all state-run schools in New Zealand.

Cultural mix

Maori culture is an important part of modern New Zealand culture. Seventy-five per cent of Maori can still name their *iwi* (tribe), and Maori language, customs, songs and dances are taught in all state-run schools. Official government documents are produced in both Maori and English. Mixed marriages mean that large numbers of New Zealanders identify with both cultures, as opera star Kiri Te Kanawa does. And many of the country's leading modern artists are descendants from both Maori and ***pakeha*** (non-Maori) ancestors. Five of New Zealand's 60 **electoral seats** are reserved for Maori, so they have a voice in the national parliament. In these ways, aspects of traditional and modern Maori culture have become mainstream.

Keeping clean

A key moment in New Zealand's cultural history was the Labour Government's decision, in 1984, to refuse entry into New Zealand ports to nuclear-powered or armed ships. This policy has proved hugely popular and adds to the people's image of inhabiting the world's cleanest and greenest country. In an effort to keep it that way, many of New Zealand's farmers are introducing **organic** growing methods and resisting the introduction of **genetically modified** foods.

Winds of change

Until recently, the dance, music and drama scene in New Zealand followed the British tradition. The Royal New Zealand Ballet Company played to the wealthy few, the opera attracted the usual buffs and theatre meant a stiff and formal night out. Not any more. New Zealand today is known for its fresh, unusual and experimental approach to the performing arts. Performances celebrate the country's new-found sense of **diversity** and often challenge audiences with confronting issues.

Music

Where else in the world would a CD of Scottish bagpipe music (*Skirl*) share the charts with Chinese-Maori pop star Bic Runga's hit album *Drive*? New Zealand has produced many internationally recognised musicians, many of whom are contributing to the revival of the music scene in the main music centres of Auckland, Wellington and Dunedin.

Dame Kiri Te Kanawa was already a well-known opera star when she sang at the wedding of Prince Charles and Diana Spencer in London in 1981 to an audience of over 600 million. Born in 1944 of Maori and Irish parents, but adopted soon afterwards, Dame Kiri became an overnight sensation in 1971 when she sang at the Royal Opera House in Covent Garden, London. She is one of the best-known opera singers in the world, but still returns frequently to New Zealand. Her performance on the beach of her home town, Gisborne, to greet the new millennium was beamed to 55 countries around the world.

Dame Kiri Te Kanawa is one of the best known opera singers in the world.

The internationally successful band Pacifier

Equally loved in New Zealand is the opera singer Dame Malvina Major. Her winning personality showed up at her debut at the age of three, when she gatecrashed her brothers' and sisters' stage performance, to the delight of the audience. Her voice is hailed by critics around the world.

Pop and rock scene

Modern music is alive and well in New Zealand. A legend in Australia and their home country, singer–songwriters Neil Finn and his brother Tim became famous in the 1970s with their band Split Enz. Neil Finn's band, Crowded House, was also wildly popular during the 1980s, and their hit *Don't Dream it's Over* is a classic. As a solo performer, Neil Finn commands respect for his sensitive lyrics and enduring music.

For 20 years, Dave Dobbyn's band DD Smash rocked the New Zealand charts. Hits include the classics *Whaling* and *Outlook for Thursday*. His soundtrack themes *Slice of Heaven* and *Oughta Be in Love*, written for the film of the cartoon *Footrot Flats*, also became classics. His 1994 album *Twist* featured Neil and Tim Finn, and Don McGlashan from the Muttonbirds. Dave Dobbyn sees his country as Polynesian, a view he shares with highly successful singer–songwriter Bic Runga. Her striking Chinese-Maori looks and vocal talent have made *Drive* (1997) the biggest selling New Zealand album in history. Other internationally successful bands include Weta, Pacifier (peviously known as Shihad), and Moana and the Moa Hunters.

On the stage

Murder and violence are common subjects in New Zealand arts, and the play, *Verbatim* (1992) by William Brandt and Miranda Harcourt, continues the trend. This disturbing play explores the true story of the infamous Aaron Daly murder case through the actual words of convicted murderers and victims' families. It achieved success in London, Edinburgh and New York. Follow-up plays in the same style include *Touch and Go* and *Portraits*.

Miranda Harcourt is also one of the country's most popular stage, film and TV actors. Her special interest in drama as **therapy** led her to perform *Verbatim* in every prison in New Zealand, as well as in psychiatric hospitals. The New York run of the play starred Giarna Te Kanawa, whose performance of all six parts brought her international success. Giarna is a cousin of famous opera singer, Kiri Te Kanawa.

Maori dance is performed at many important and social gatherings.

Dance

Every kind of social dance is available in New Zealand's larger centres, from **retro** and disco to ballroom and traditional cultural dances. Irish and Scottish folk dance are also big in the South Island. But it is in classical and contemporary dance that New Zealand really shines.

The Royal New Zealand Ballet, based in Wellington, is the country's leading ballet company. It has updated its image in recent years with the appointment of innovative dancer–**choreographer** Douglas Wright. He is known for his challenging and controversial works like *Buried Venus* (1996), and has made several dance films with director Chris Graves. New Zealand's most famous ballet dancer is Sir Jon Trimmer. Known worldwide for roles in traditional ballets like *Petrouchka*, he has belonged to the Royal New Zealand Ballet company for over 40 years. In 1999 he was awarded a knighthood for his services to ballet.

The Royal New Zealand Ballet is the country's leading ballet company.

Modern dance

Modern dance thrives in New Zealand's lively arts scene. The BlackGrace Dance Company, established in Auckland in 1995, is an all-male group of mainly Maori and Pacific Islander dancers. Their blend of traditional and contemporary dance with a South Pacific flavour has proven a hit at home and in Australia.

Curve is an all-women's modern dance company founded by choreographer Karen Barbour to promote the art of dance for women. The company's performances include images projected onto screens, live and electronic music, and stories reflecting women's experiences.

Similarly innovative is the company Touch Compass, which includes dancers with disabilities that range from Down's Syndrome to **paraplegia**. The company specialises in airborne acts, with performers using harnesses, wheelchairs and even scooters in mid-air. Touch Compass performed at the Sydney Paralympic Games in 2000.

International success

Everyone recognises the famous Maori *haka* chant-dance traditionally performed before battle. *Kapa haka* group Pounamu Kai Tahu performed *haka* and *poi* dances at the dawn opening ceremony of the world-famous Venice Biennale Arts festival, in 2001. They received rave reviews from critics.

11

MAORI ARTS

Ancient times

Aotearoa (land of the long white cloud), the Maoris say, was formed at the dawn of time when ancestor Maui went fishing in his canoe and pulled up a huge fish from the ocean depths. The fish became the North Island, his canoe the South Island, and the small island down south (Stewart Island) was the canoe's anchor. Long afterwards, in about AD 800, legendary seafarer Kupe sailed from his island home, Hawaiki, and discovered these islands. His descendants are the Maori people of today.

Unique creativity

Intricate swirls, lines, and animal and human figures are carved by master-craftspeople.

New Zealand is colder and wetter than the early Polynesians' former island homes. It has few metals, except gold, and is a long way from ancient trading routes. So the Maori found new ways of making and decorating the things they needed: meeting houses (*marae*), canoes (*waka*), musical instruments, fishing gear, tools, weapons, clothes and jewellery. Using what was available, early Maoris made bone and stone tools, used greenstone (*pounamu*) for jewellery and weapons, processed plants like **flax** (*harakeke*) for weaving, and used feathers and dog skin for clothing. This adaptability led to the Maori's unique skill and creativity in visual arts. Without writing, history and folklore were remembered in oral histories (*whakapapa*), songs (*waiata*) and dances (*haka*). All these art forms were part of Maori daily life.

For 150 years after European settlement, many of these traditional arts declined, but since the 1970s there has been a revival of Maori arts and crafts. Now, all over the islands, Maori are rediscovering their cultural roots and learning the skills and values of their ancestors once again.

❋ Carving

Maori carving is among the best in the world. Carved greenstone *tiki* (charms) were thought to bring power to the wearer, hair was kept in place with decorated bone combs, and fighting clubs (*patu*) were shaped into elegant curves by master-craftspeople. Intricate swirls, lines, and animal and human figures also decorated the prows of canoes (*waka*). The best wood for these long boats is totara and, even today, special rituals accompany the tree-felling and building tasks. Boat builders, carvers and the canoes were traditionally *tapu* (sacred). Today, *waka* may be built from wood, laminated timber or fibreglass and used for special cultural events. In 1990, several large war canoes (*waka taua*) were built to celebrate the 150th anniversary of the signing of the famous Treaty of Waitangi in 1840, which recognised Maori land rights.

Many *iwi* (tribes) have a *whare whakairo* (carved meeting house), which is their spiritual home. Rafters, wall panels and entrance are richly carved, often with mask-like human faces with huge eyes and tongues sticking out. The *wharenui* (meeting house), and the flat space in front (*maraeatea*) where ceremonies are held, are sacred and treated with great respect. One of New Zealand's most famous *wharenui* is Te Hau Ki Turanga meeting house. It is housed in Te Papa Tongarewa, the national Museum, but new ones are still being built.

Carved *tiki* (charms) were thought to bring power to the wearer.

Women's arts

Legend tells how the art of weaving (*raranga*) was given to Maori women by a fairy named *Niwareka* who made the first cloak. Traditionally, cloth was made from flax which the women gathered, soaked in water, pounded then bleached. Short skirts (*piupiu*) for men and women were made of strands of curled flax. Headbands and mats were also woven. Cloaks (*kakahu*) were often made of dogs' skins or feathers, and were beautifully decorated with hanging strands of braid, dogs' fur and fringes. New Zealand's most famous weaver and artist was Dame Rangimarie Hetet (1892–1995), who has rooms in Te Papa Tongarewa museum named after her.

Tukutuku is the craft of making woven reed panels. Inside walls were lined with these panels, which were stitched with patterns and hung between carved figures of the ancestors in the *wharenui* (meeting houses). Women also made the *poi* balls for the famous *poi* dance. Unique to New Zealand, this is a graceful women's dance where performers hold balls on short strings and twirl them in time to the music.

Moko revival

Tattoos (*moko*) were traditionally applied with sharpened bone needles, a hammer and blue dye. It is no wonder only high-ranking chiefs sported them. Women's *moko* were applied on the lips and chin and sometimes the arms, but men had tattoos covering the whole face and buttocks. Traditional designs were swirls and lines, not pictures. There has been a huge rise in interest in tattoos in the last ten years.

14 **Skirts for men and women are traditionally made of strands of curled flax.**

A Maori handbag woven from native flax leaves

A painting by Maori artist Peter Robinson entitled *Painting 1993*. The artist used tar, wax and oil on canvas.

Modern Maori *moko* artists take their work very seriously. *Moko* artist Rangi Skipper is also a sculptor in wood, stone, bone and shell, and makes traditional musical instruments including nose flutes made of whale's teeth. He views *moko* as proud symbols of Maori belonging. Even with modern tattooing instruments, the process is painful. A woman's chin and lip tattoo takes around six hours to apply. Large tattoos take much longer.

New wave artists

The 1990s saw a new wave of Maori art, not traditional but city-based, hard-hitting, and challenging people's views of Maori culture. Such artists include Lisa Reihana, whose animated short film *Wog Features* (1990) combines live action, cartoons and rap music to give a comic spin on race relations. She performed with the group of artists, Pacific Sisters, at the Sydney Biennale Arts Festival 2000, which included island dancers in 'grass' skirts made of video tape. Peter Robinson's and Jacqueline Fraser's artworks use odd collections of objects put together to create artistic statements. Alan Duff's violent, disturbing novels tell of the bitterness and hopelessness some Maori feel when they have been alienated from their traditional cultural values. His novel *Once Were Warriors* was a best-seller in New Zealand.

FASHION

Islands of style

New Zealanders are now among the world leaders in fashion design. They are admired for their inventiveness and creativity, nurtured through a tradition of making do with what is available. In 1998, Karen Walker caused a sensation at Australian Fashion Week in Sydney with her wearable, flattering and original designs. Others like Kate Sylvester, Collette Dinnegan, Helen Cherry and Marilyn Sainty have also achieved international success. High fashion is typically a male **domain**, but in New Zealand women dominate the industry and take out most of the awards. Fashion is big business, too, employing over 1600 people in Auckland alone and bringing $NZ100 million in export earnings each year. The first New Zealand Fashion Week, held in October 2001, showcased over 100 local designers.

Traditional dress

Traditionally, Maori men and women wore 'grass' skirts made of strands of dried flax (*harakeke*), which was dyed with clay into patterns. Headbands (*tipare*) were decorated with geometric designs, often in red, black and white. Women's tops called *pari* were similarly patterned, each design indicating their **kinship** group. A long cloak (*korowai*) made of flax was worn for warmth and special ceremonies. *Korowai* were often beautifully decorated with feathers and fringes. Face tattoos used to be applied with sharpened wooden needles, but today a pen is sometimes used.

Modern interpretations of traditional dress are showcased in the annual Pasifika Fashion Awards, established in 1993 for islanders living in New Zealand. Styles build on traditional materials and reinvent them for modern wear.

Traditional Maori dress

Wearable art

Body suits made of telephones, dresses made of onion skins and fake grass – it could only happen at the Wearable Art Awards! Held every September in Nelson, this four-night **extravaganza** of creativity and fun is now an international event. Garments are designed by sculptors, artists, fabric designers, school children and even nursing-home residents. Categories include a Bizarre Bra section (where recent entries featured fish bowls and soccer balls), and official entry forms state 'no garments to exceed 3 metres in height'! The happy mix of art, fashion and humour captures the essence of New Zealand's originality.

Gallery of fashion

Wellington's vast national museum, Te Papa Tongarewa (commonly referred to as 'Te Papa'), now includes a gallery of fashion. Modern New Zealand designs, including Maori and Pacific Islander fashion, are displayed. Samoan Paula Chan's unique contemporary wedding dress is made entirely of *tapa* cloth (processed bark) and decorated with traditional fly whisk (*sennit*) braiding. One of the most popular exhibits is the original costume worn by Xena, Warrior Princess in the famous TV adventure fantasy series made in New Zealand.

Flushed with fashion

Among Auckland's High Street clothes boutiques, a renovated toilet block has taken on a fashion theme. Artist Cathryn Monro has decorated external walls with giant dress patterns, and embedded fabrics, zips and belts in the tiles.

17

FOOD

A shift in focus

New Zealand produces much more food than it needs. For many years, most of it was exported to England and Europe, earning easy profits. But in the early 1970s, the **European Common Market** was established, requiring member countries to buy most of their food from each other, and restricting imports. Suddenly, New Zealand had to find new buyers. Today, Australia, the United States of America, Japan and east Asia buy most of the country's food. As a result, New Zealand has shifted its focus. Once an English outpost, it now sees itself as part of the Pacific region, with its sights firmly on Asia.

In recent years, tastes have become more varied and sophisticated and dining out is a way of life, but it was not always so. Visitors in the 1950s and 1960s were dismayed at the boring, stay-at-home lifestyle of the New Zealanders. As famous English cricketer Freddy Trueman put it: 'When I went to New Zealand – it was shut'!

Nature's bounty

Rich soil, clean air and plenty of water make New Zealand a world-class food producer. Grass-fed beef is a top export, and New Zealand lamb is famous. Meats like venison (deer meat) and farmed rabbit are also exported. Seafoods and fish are very popular with locals. Bluff oysters from the southern tip of the South Island are a **delicacy**. Whitebait are tiny silver fish, deep fried in batter and eaten whole. Trout fish live in mountain rivers, but it is illegal to serve this endangered species in restaurants. Dairy cattle thrive in the cool, wet climate and New Zealand's cream, butter and cheeses are excellent.

Fresh and natural

New Zealand's **isolation** means low pollution and few diseases, so food can be grown naturally. Recent animal disease outbreaks in Europe mean many buyers will not risk getting ill by eating European meat. **Genetically modified**, artificially produced foods are also becoming unpopular throughout the world. Both these factors have raised world demand for naturally fed, disease-free meat, and **organic** fruit and vegetables. In 2000, organic fruit and vegetable exports from New Zealand topped $NZ60 million – up from only $NZ12 million in 1997 – and many farmers see organic as the way of the future.

Cooking food in a *hangi* takes more than three hours.

Maori food

Hangi traditionally marked a special Maori celebration and this method of cooking is still popular today. A *hangi* is a Maori version of cooking in an earth pit that is found throughout the South Pacific. The pit is dug around one metre deep and the earth in it is trampled flat. Layers of wood are put in it with stones placed on top, and it is set alight. As embers form, the red hot stones drop to the pit bottom, and wet leaves or sacks are put over them. Pork, chicken or beef, and *kumara* (sweet potatoes) and other vegetables are placed on top in woven flax baskets (often made of wire today). More wet leaves are put on top and the earth is shovelled back on. It takes more than three hours to cook the food, then all is dug up and served hot.

Great pavlova debate

Which country – New Zealand or Australia – invented this famous meringue dessert?

It seems both countries want a piece of the pav! In 1934, chef Bert Sachse of the Esplanade Hotel in Perth first cooked and named the meringue cake in honour of an earlier visit by the famous Russian ballerina, Anna Pavlova. But a New Zealand recipe book dated 1927 includes the famous dessert. Experts now think that New Zealanders may have invented the pavlova and that Bert Sachse refined and named it.

FILM AND *television*

◆ Pioneer filmmakers

Since 1896, when the first movie was screened in New Zealand, New Zealanders have been active in filmmaking. A.H. Whitehouse was a pioneer, travelling the country filming local events. His **newsreel** showing soldiers departing for the Boer War in 1900 is the oldest surviving New Zealand film. *Hinemoa*, made in 1914, was filmed in Rotorua and had a huge Maori cast. Rudall Heyward directed both silent and sound films including the famous *Rewi's Last Stand* about a Maori hero. Another pioneer, Edwin (Ted) Coubray, invented a unique sound film technique long before Hollywood discovered 'talkies'.

Footrot Flats

New Zealand's top grossing film for many years was an animated version of the popular local comic *Footrot Flats* by Murray Ball. Titled *The Dog's Tale*, this full-length movie featured the voice of famous comedian John Clarke as Wal. Its theme song, *Slice of Heaven* by Dave Dobbyn, has become a New Zealand classic.

◆ Revival

TV stifled local filmmaking during the 1950s and 1960s, but in the late 1970s it revived. *Sleeping Dogs*, made in 1977, launched international star Sam Neill in his acting career. New Zealand filmmakers have become famous for quirky, bleak and brooding films. *Vigil* (1984), about a young girl growing up in a remote **backwater**, gained success at the Cannes Film Festival.

Director Jane Campion's *An Angel at My Table* (1990) tells the life story of the author Janet Frame, and *The Piano* (1993) won the top prize at the Cannes Film Festival and three **Oscars**, bringing world attention to New Zealand films.

Maori filmmaker Lee Tamahori showed a violent, brutal world in his 1994 film about urban Maori, *Once Were Warriors*. It remains the most successful New Zealand film ever made. Peter Jackson also explored the theme of violence in his 1994 film *Heavenly Creatures*, based on a true story about two schoolgirls who committed murder. He has gained publicity recently as the maker of the huge-budget film version of *Lord of the Rings* (2001), shot in New Zealand.

Lucy Lawless as Xena, Warrior Princess

Television

New Zealand struggles to fund local TV programs, and its four main channels are swamped with US- and British-made productions. However, some local programs have made a big impact.

Shortland Street is a TV hospital drama series. Now in its tenth year, it attracts 700 000 viewers nightly in New Zealand and also has an international audience in the UK, South Africa, Australia and the Pacific nations. The show has the usual mix of dramatic crises and love interests but has gained respect for its treatment of difficult topics like AIDS and youth suicide. Actors in the show are from a number of ethnic backgrounds and have achieved hero status.

Another hero is Xena, Warrior Princess. Leading actor Lucy Lawless was born in Auckland and has become world famous for her role as the feisty Xena in the fantasy series of the same name. Children's shows like *What Now?*, *Squirtworld* and the Maori preschool show *Tikitiki* cater for younger tastes.

BOOKS

New Zealand has produced many world-renowned writers. Best known internationally is Katherine Mansfield (1888–1923) whose short stories tell about growing up in Wellington (*Prelude and At the Bay*).

Janet Frame was born in Dunedin in 1924 into a poor family. Her autobiographical novels *To the Is-Land* (1982), *An Angel at My Table* (1984) and the *Envoy from Mirror City* (1985) were made into a successful film by world-famous New Zealand director, Jane Campion.

Patricia Grace makes strong use of Maori traditions and language in her books, which include the novel *Potiki* and the famous short piece *Between Earth and Sky*. Another Maori writer, Keri Hulme, was a complete unknown until her first novel *the bone people* (1983) won the international Booker Prize. Her later books have not matched this early success. Witi Ihimaera is widely admired for stories such as *The Matriarch* (1986) and *The Whale Rider* (1987), about a young girl's relationship with a whale. The most famous and controversial Maori writer is Alan Duff whose novels *Once Were Warriors* and *One Night Out Stealing* tell of violence in modern, urban Maori families. He is a powerful figure and very active in social issues.

Poetry

The country's most respected Maori poet writing in English is Hone Tuwhare. His first collection titled *No Ordinary Sun* (1964) is still read in schools. In 1999 he was honoured for his work by being named New Zealand Te Mata **Poet Laureate**.

James K. Baxter, Dennis Glover and Allen Curnow are famous *pakeha* poets. One of the most popular poets in the country is the eccentric Sam Hunt. His **larrikin** style belies the emotional depth and sensitivity of his poems. He writes about familiar subjects like his sheepdog, Minstrel (in *Bow Wow Poems*) and his troubled relationship with his father. Sam Hunt has read his poems to the New Zealand parliament, and performed with legendary rock band Split Enz.

Nothing to worry about

Alan Duff is best known for his adult novel, *Once Were Warriors*, but he is also passionate about kids and reading. His charity 'Books in Homes' has donated one million books to disadvantaged school children. Now he has written a children's book, *Once Were Worriers*, about spiders, snakes, scary faces and bullies – a humorous look at all the things kids worry about.

New Zealand author–illustrator Lynley Dodd created the much loved character Hairy McClary from Donaldson's Dairy.

Written for children

Gwenda Turner is popular among preschoolers for her colourful, realistic illustrations of toddlers' daily lives. Margaret Mahy writes complex, well-crafted novels for youngsters and teenagers. She has been awarded the international Carnegie Medal twice, for *The Haunting* and *The Changeover*.

Famous adult author Patricia Grace reveals Maori life in her preschoolers' picture books such as *Kimi and the Watermelon*. Dorothy Butler, a librarian, has inspired generations of parents to read to their children with her famous text *Babies Need Books*.

New Zealand's best-loved comic strip is Murray Ball's *Footrot Flats*. Its off-beat humour and lively characters have delighted readers of daily newspapers across the country since 1975.

THE ROLE
of women

A woman's place

In New Zealand, a woman's place is definitely not in the home. No other country has so many women in positions of power. The Chief Justice of the High Court is Dame Sian Elias, appointed in 1999, and the Governor-General is Dame Sylvia Cartwright. Helen Clark is New Zealand's second female Prime Minister. She took over from Jenny Shipley who was leader of the conservative opposition. The country's Attorney-General and Minister for Labour is the lawyer and leading feminist, Margaret Wilson. In all, women make up 30 per cent of the national Parliament and have a proud history of political activity. Nevertheless, New Zealand women on average still earn 25 per cent less than men.

Pioneer feminist

Kate Sheppard led the fight for women to be allowed to vote in New Zealand. Born in England in 1847 and immigrating to New Zealand as a child, she organised meetings, lobbied politicians and raised a petition of 32 000 signatures supporting women's voting rights. She even persuaded conservative politician Sir John Hall to help her. Finally, on 19 September 1893, women over 21 were given the vote. New Zealand was the first country in the world in which all women had that right. Kate Sheppard went on to establish the *White Ribbon*, the first New Zealand newspaper written and run entirely by women.

Helen Clark is New Zealand's second female Prime Minister.

The Black Ferns rugby team performing the *haka* dance before a game

 ## Maori women

Fifteen per cent of all females in New Zealand are Maori. In areas of health, education and employment they do less well than their non-Maori sisters, but they are gaining ground. Life expectancy is around 74 years (five years lower than for non-Maori women) and they have twice as many children and are more likely to suffer poor health from smoking, diabetes and heart disease.

However, Maori women's health has steadily improved since 1950, and they are remaining at school longer (rates of girls completing school are up 250 per cent since 1986). Almost half (47 per cent) of all Maori women are in paid work, but Maori families suffered more than others from the economic hardships of the 1980s, and incomes are lower than for non-Maori women.

The Black Ferns

Rugby is one of the toughest sports around, as fans of the famous New Zealand All-Blacks know. Now women are getting into the **scrum** and beating the men at their own game. The Black Ferns, New Zealand's national women's rugby team, are 2001 World Champions.

ARTS AND CRAFTS

Artistic innovators

Every kind of visual art is practised in New Zealand: painting, sculpture, pottery, jewellery-making, weaving, photography and more. Perhaps because of the country's isolation, New Zealand's artists are not afraid to break new ground. Many experiment with new forms and materials and challenge ordinary people's understanding of what art should be.

Modernist painters

Colin McCahon (1919–1987) is New Zealand's most famous artist. Known as a modernist painter, his religious pictures produced howls of protest in the 1940s because they included soap powder packets, comic book characters and speech bubbles. Often dark and brooding, his abstract pictures include writing, numbers, signs and messages. In later life he became one of New Zealand's most respected artists, and he is well known internationally.

Another artist who uses words and signs in his paintings is Maori modernist painter Ralph Hotere. Born in 1931, Hotere lived for five years in Europe and combines western art styles with Maori symbols. One of New Zealand's most famous artists, he is known for his use of unusual materials like corrugated iron, stainless steel, loose canvas – and number 8 fencing wire! He also worked with well-known Maori poet Hone Tuwhare to produce some of New Zealand's best-loved books of poetry. Hotere is extremely quiet and retiring. A documentary about him by filmmaker Merata Mita took seven years to make.

Photography

Photographer Fiona Pardington became known for her dramatic and complex images when well-known fashion designer Collette Dinnegan asked her to produce the cover for her 2000 catalogue. The result, *Dark Angel*, brought Pardington international attention. Of Scottish and Maori parents, she is also known for her photographs of homeless people and drug addicts. A recent exhibition was based on a set of prints found in a rubbish skip.

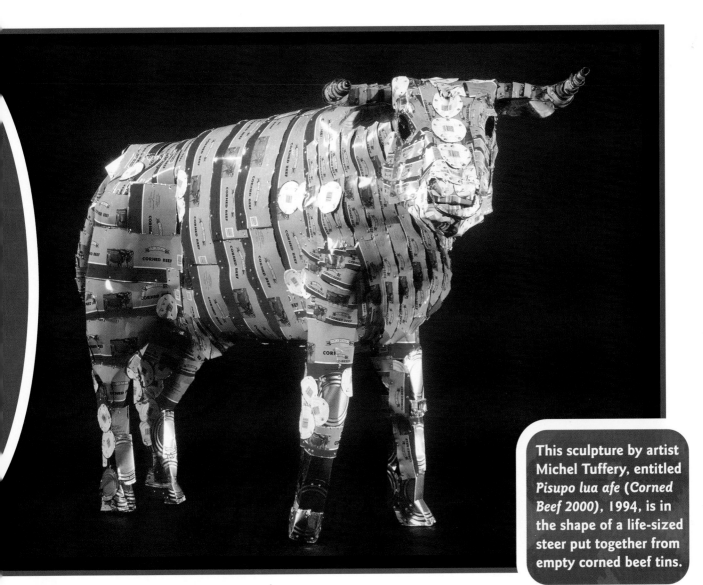

This sculpture by artist Michel Tuffery, entitled *Pisupo lua afe (Corned Beef 2000)*, 1994, is in the shape of a life-sized steer put together from empty corned beef tins.

New young artists

Two modern artists pushing the boundaries are Jacqueline Fraser and Peter Robinson. Both part-Maori, they use a wide variety of materials in unusual ways to create **mixed media installations**. Jacqueline Fraser uses fabrics, electrical wire, ribbons, weaving and braiding to express her Maori background and her interest in dress and fashion as an artform. Peter Robinson is widely admired for his innovative ideas. One exhibition has been described as 'a cluttered trade shop draped with carpets, littered with … knick-knacks'! He has an international reputation and is exhibited in the national museum, Te Papa. Both Fraser and Robinson represented New Zealand in 2001 in the important international arts festival, the Venice Biennale.

Beauty in ordinary things

Rosalie Gascoigne did not paint or draw but was one of the country's best-loved artists. She was born in New Zealand in 1917 but lived most of her life in Australia. Her beautiful works are collages of ordinary objects including road signs, grasses, sticks and bits of lino.

Creative crafts

Glowing red **jasper**, creamy pearl-shell and greenstone are used by Warwick Freeman to make his unusual and exquisite jewellery. His simple, pared-down designs and use of distinctive, South Pacific materials make him New Zealand's leading contemporary jeweller. His work is in galleries around the world.

With 50 million sheep, it is no wonder that New Zealanders are keen workers in wool. Spinning, weaving and felting are popular crafts. Felt is becoming an art form, with sculptures and hung artworks being shown in galleries around the country. Maeve Harrison's felt 'painting' *Fox River*, with its blending of layers and subtle shades of blue, has the look of a watercolour painting. It was awarded top prize in the Creative Fibre National Exhibition in Wellington in 2001.

Furniture-maker Greg Bloomfield's funky bed, *Noah's Tipsy*, reflects the lively craft scene in New Zealand.

New Zealand's vast natural forests have some of the best woodworking timber in the world, including kauri and hoop pine, beech and myrtle. The Maori are world famous for their carving skills, but modern artists in wood are also making a name for themselves. Greg Bloomfield makes quirky, brightly painted furniture with odd angles and decorative features like his *Jester* – a child's desk that looks like a clown.

Kawakawa's famous public toilets designed by artist Friedensreich Hundertwasser

Architecture

Auckland's Sky Tower is the tallest building in the Southern Hemisphere, but New Zealanders are not widely known for outstanding architecture. The national parliament building in Wellington instantly gained the nickname 'The Beehive' for its squat, rounded shape.

The need to make buildings earthquake-proof on New Zealand's unstable ground has helped determine building styles. Thousands flock to admire the towns of Napier and Hastings on Hawke Bay in the North Island. In 1931 a violent earthquake measuring 7.9 on the **Richter scale** hit the area and flattened both cities. The **upthrust** of the quake created an extra 40 square kilometres of land from former seabed. Both towns were fully rebuilt in the famous **Art Deco** style, and represent the best examples of that type of architecture in the world. Now a major tourist centre, Napier conducts quake and Art Deco tours.

Toilet art

If you use the public toilets in the small town of Kawakawa you are in for an artistic experience. Artist Friedensreich Hundertwasser donated these astonishing facilities to its citizens. Features include windows made of wine bottles, leaf-printed flagstones, technicolour mosaic tiles and stained glass whales. He even ordered that all the vegetation removed from the building site be replanted – on the roof!

29

GLOSSARY

Art Deco   a decorative style of the 1920s and 1930s

backwater   out-of-the-way; an old-fashioned place

choreographer   a person who designs and creates dances

delicacy   very special to eat

diversity   variety, difference

domain   an area of action or interest

electoral seats   elected positions for politicians in the parliament

endurance races   very difficult races that test competitors to the limit

European Common Market   an organisation controlling trade between a group of European countries

extravaganza   extravagant or showy event

flax   a grass-like plant used to make cloth

genetically modified   plants or animals whose characteristics have been altered by scientists

isolation   being alone or apart

jasper   a semi-precious stone

kinship   family relationship

larrikin   rowdy and carefree

mixed media installations   unusual sculptures or other works of art that have been created using a variety of materials

multicultural   a mix of people from many different countries and cultures

newsreel   a short film presenting current news events

nuclear-powered   using uranium, a radioactive fuel

organic   (food) grown without harmful chemicals

Oscars   awards given in the USA for excellence in films; officially known as the Academy Awards

pakeha   the Maori word for non-Maori people

Poet Laureate   honour awarded to a poet by the government; official government poet

Polynesian   from the area that includes the Hawaiian Islands, Easter Island and the major island groups Samoa, Cook, Line, Tonga and French Polynesia

republic   a state ruled by the people or their representatives

retro   in the style of the 1950s–1980s

Richter scale   scale (invented by a man named Richter) used to measure the severity of earthquakes

scrum   (in rugby) a tight mass of players with the ball in the middle

therapy   (medical) treatment

upthrust   upwards push of the earth

FURTHER *information*

Books

Ercelawn, A. *Countries of the World* series – *New Zealand*. Times Editions, Singapore, 2001.

First Peoples series – *Maori of New Zealand*. Times Editions, Singapore, 2001.

Guile, M. *Australia's Neighbours* series – *New Zealand*. Heinemann Library, Melbourne, 2000.

Yip, D. and A. Ercelawn. *Welcome to My Country* series – *Welcome to New Zealand*. Times Editions, Singapore, 2001

Websites

Auckland Art Gallery (Toi o Tamaki): www.akcity.govt.nz/around/places/artgallery/index.html

Museum of New Zealand (Te Papa Tongarewa):   www.tepapa.govt.nz

Textile arts: www.textiles.org.nz

INDEX